Stock Market Investing for Beginners

Learn Stocks Investing Essentials to Make Money

by S. M. Rambhia

Published by:
S. M. Rambhia

© Copyright 2014 – S. M. Rambhia

ISBN-13: 978-1505685138
ISBN-10: 1505685133

ALL RIGHTS RESERVED. No part of this publication may be reproduced or transmitted in any form whatsoever, electronic, or mechanical, including photocopying, recording, or by any informational storage or retrieval system without express written, dated and signed permission from the author.

Table of Contents

Introduction 7

Chapter 1: INVESTMENT BASICS 9
What is Investment? 9
Why should one invest? 9
When to Start Investing? 10
Eleven Important Steps of Investment: 11

Chapter 2: TYPES OF INVESTMENT 12
Stocks 12
Bonds 12
Real estate 13
Foreign currency 13
Mutual Funds 13
Certificates of Deposit, or CDs 14
Life Insurance 14
Savings accounts 14

Chapter 3: INTRODUCTION TO STOCKS 15
The Definition of a Stock 15
Stock Owner 15
What is meant by a Stock Exchange? 16
What is an 'Equity'/Share? 16
What is a 'Debt Instrument'? 16
What is a Derivative? 17
What is a Mutual Fund? 17
What is an Index? 18
What is a Depository? 18
Types Of Stocks 19
Common Stock 19

Preferred Stock 20

Chapter 4: STOCK MARKET EXCHANGE 21
    The New York Stock Exchange 22
    The NASDAQ 23
    Bombay Stock Exchange (BSE) 24
    Other Exchanges 25

Chapter 5: THE BULLS, THE BEARS AND THE FARM 26
    The Bulls 26
    The Bears 27
    The Other Animals on the Farm - Chickens and Pigs 27
    What Type of Investor Will You Be? 28

Chapter 6: THE ABC OF STOCK MARKET JARGON 29
    (a) "The market is up 100 points today" 29
    (b) "The market is crashing" or "The market is rallying" 30
    (c) Market Timing 30
    (d) A "Tick" 31
    (e) Double-Dip 31
    (f) Paper-Trading 31
    (g) "Quantitative Easing will bolster the economy" 32
    (h) "Analysts raise outlook for company" 32

Chapter 7: HOW TO READ A STOCK TABLE/QUOTE 34
    Quotes on the Internet 36

Chapter 8: STOCK MARKET FORECASTING

.... **38**
    Fundamental Analysis 39
    Technical Analysis 39

Chapter 9: FUNDAMENTALS FOR INVESTORS
.... **41**
    Stock Analyzing 42
    Fundamentalists 43

Chapter 10: WHAT CAUSES STOCK PRICES TO CHANGE? **51**
    Complexity of the Process 51
    High Investor Confidence Raises Price 52
    Decisions Made Based on Perceptions 52
    Supply/Demand of Stock 53

Chapter 11: HOW TO FIND GOOD STOCKS - 3 PROVEN STEPS **55**
    Dividend Stocks 56
    Long Term Growth 56
    Financial Statements 56
    Do you know which ones to avoid? 57

Chapter 12: POWER OF DIVERSIFICATION 61
    What is Diversification? 61
    Two Types of Risk 63
    Some Benefits of having Diversified Portfolio
.... 63
    WHY DIVERSIFICATION IS SO IMPORTANT? . 64

Chapter 13: READY TO BEGIN INVESTING? 67
Chapter 14: COMMON MISTAKES THAT NEWBIES MAKE **70**

Chapter 15: HOW TO BECOME STOCKS GENIUS 74
    Don't be fool- never buy dead stocks 74
    Research is the key to success 74
    Always invest in stocks that have good liquidity 75
    Determine the undervalue stocks and positions in them 76
    Market watch 76
    Effective planning 76
    Check for stocks from reputed companies 77

Chapter 16: EXPLORE YOUR STOCKS KNOWLEDGE - QUIZ 78
    Answer Key 82

Chapter 17: Basic Terminologies 85
    Glossary for Beginners 87

Introduction

Clueless about how or even why to invest in stock market? Don't worry. In this book you will learn not only about what stock market is but you will get useful information and guidance about how you should prepare yourself before entering this battle of bulls and bears and emerge victorious. This book is designed to be precise about informing a newbee about stock market without confusing with excessive information that might get too heavy for a beginner and demotivate him even before stepping in the market. I have tried to clarify some of the overhyped jargons used in the market. Discover ways which will help you find good stocks and avoid common mistakes often made by investors. Take the quiz to explore your stocks knowledge after reading this book. All the answers to the quiz are explained in detail in case you get lost somewhere. You will find a Glossary along with the basic terminologies used in stock market in Ch17 at the end of the book. You can refer it incase you get stuck somewhere.

Lets Get Started..!!!

Chapter 1:
INVESTMENT BASICS

What is Investment?

The money you earn is partly spent and the rest saved for meeting future expenses. Instead of keeping the savings idle you may like to use savings in order to get return on it in the future. This is called Investment.

Why should one invest?

One needs to invest to:
- Earn return on your idle resources.
- Generate a specified sum of money for a specific goal in life.
- Make a provision for an uncertain future.

One of the important reasons why one needs to invest wisely is to meet the cost of Inflation. Inflation is the rate at which the cost of living increases. The cost of living is simply what it costs to buy the goods and services you need to live. Inflation causes money to lose value because it will not buy the same amount of a good or a service in the future as it does now or did in the past. For example, if there was a 6% inflation rate for the next 20 years, a Rs. 100 purchase today would cost Rs. 321 in 20 years. This is why it is important to consider inflation as a factor in any long-term investment strategy. Remember to look at an investment's 'real' rate of return, which is the return after inflation. The aim of investments should be to provide a return above the inflation rate to ensure that the investment does not decrease in value. For example, if the annual inflation rate is 6%, then the investment will need to earn more than 6% to ensure it increases in value. If the after-tax return on your investment is less than the inflation rate, then your assets have actually decreased in value; that is, they won't buy as much today as they did last year.

When to Start Investing?

The sooner one starts investing the better. By investing early you allow your investments more time to grow, whereby the concept of compounding (as we shall see later) increases your income, by accumulating the principal and the interest or dividend earned on it, year after year.

The three golden rules for all investors are:
- Invest early
- Invest regularly
- Invest for long term and not short term

Eleven Important Steps of Investment:

1. Obtain written documents explaining the investment.
2. Read and understand such documents.
3. Verify the legitimacy of the investment.
4. Find out the costs and benefits associated with the investment.
5. Assess the risk-return profile of the investment.
6. Know the liquidity and safety aspects of the investment.
7. Ascertain if it is appropriate for your specific goals.
8. Compare these details with other investment opportunities available.
9. Examine if it fits in with other investments you are considering or you have already made deal only through an authorized intermediary.
10. Seek all clarifications about the intermediary and the investment.
11. Explore the options available to you if something were to go wrong, and then, if satisfied, make the investment.

Chapter 2:
TYPES OF INVESTMENT

Stocks

Stocks are buying a portion of a company or corporation. You'll become a stockholder of that company. Thus, you have your own rights there. You can gain profit with this type of investment by receiving stock dividends from that corporation. Another way of gaining profit in this is to buy low-amount stocks and then sell it in a higher price. Stocks are also considered as high-risk investment.

Bonds

Investing in bonds is like lending money. Usually it is done to a government agency. Because of that, the risk in this type of investment is lesser than stocks.

Real estate

Real estate investing is buying a property and then selling it in a higher price soon. Some real estate investors do not sell their property. They just use it for rental. That's why the flow of money to them is continuous but not that massive money like re-selling it. We are now in a buyer's market so it's better if you'll buy properties today and then re-sell it when the time changes into seller's market.

Foreign currency

Foreign currency is one of the types of investment in foreign exchange (FOREX) deals with currency trading market. It is always open and can be accessed through the use of internet. With this type of investment, you'll need to trade currency pairs for other currency pairs in the hope that you will trade for currency that has more value.

Mutual Funds

Regarding the mutual funds, when you invest on this, you will need to join a group of people who also invest in mutual funds. Basically, you and the others share the cost of hiring a professional to manage your assets, and most mutual funds include a variety of different investments, such as high-risk, long-term, short-term, stocks, bonds, and the like.

Certificates of Deposit, or CDs

CDs are alike to savings accounts, except they pay better interest. The reason for the higher interest rate is simple: when you open a CD at your local financial institution, you agree to leave the money there for a set amount of time; generally, the shortest amount of time is six months, but you may agree to a term of one year, two years, or even five years. The longer you agree to keep the CD, the higher the interest rate.

Life Insurance

Some people choose to use life insurance as an investment. Many policies have investment properties, and an insurance agent or financial advisor can help you choose which the right one is.

Savings accounts

Savings accounts offer very little return. In fact, despite they are technically a form of investment, they barely qualify anymore. They are certainly a very good way to teach your kids the process of saving though.

Those are just some of the diverse types of investment. You may also invest in a business. Invest in a company that's just starting up or invest in your own business.

Chapter 3:
INTRODUCTION TO STOCKS

The Definition of a Stock

Plain and simple, stock is a share in the ownership of a company. Stock represents a claim on the company's assets and earnings. As you acquire more stock, your ownership stake in the company becomes greater. Whether you say shares, equity, or stock, it all means the same thing.

Stock Owner

Holding a company's stock means that you are one of the many owners (shareholders) of a company and, as such, you have a claim (albeit usually very small) to everything the company owns. This means that technically you own a tiny sliver of every piece of furniture, every trademark, and every contract of the company. As an owner, you are entitled to your share of the company's earnings as well as any voting rights attached to the stock.

What is meant by a Stock Exchange?

The Securities Contract (Regulation) Act, 1956 [SCRA] defines 'Stock Exchange' as anybody of individuals, whether incorporated or not, constituted for the purpose of assisting, regulating or controlling the business of buying, selling or dealing in securities. Stock exchange could be a regional stock exchange whose area of operation/jurisdiction is specified at the time of its recognition or national exchanges, which are permitted to have nationwide trading since inception. NSE was incorporated as a national stock exchange.

What is an 'Equity'/Share?

Total equity capital of a company is divided into equal units of small denominations, each called a share. For example, in a company the total equity capital of Rs 2,00,00,000 is divided into 20,00,000 units of Rs 10 each. Each such unit of Rs 10 is called a Share. Thus, the company then is said to have 20,00,000 equity shares of Rs 10 each. The holders of such shares are members of the company and have voting rights.

What is a 'Debt Instrument'?

Debt instrument represents a contract whereby one

party lends money to another on pre-determined terms with regards to rate and periodicity of interest, repayment of principal amount by the borrower to the lender. In the Indian securities markets, the term 'bond' is used for debt instruments issued by the Central and State governments and public sector organizations and the term 'debenture' is used for instruments issued by private corporate sector.

What is a Derivative?

Derivative is a product whose value is derived from the value of one or more basic variables, called underlying. The underlying asset can be equity, index, foreign exchange (forex), commodity or any other asset. Derivative products initially emerged as hedging devices against fluctuations in commodity prices and commodity-linked derivatives remained the sole form of such products for almost three hundred years. The financial derivatives came into spotlight in post-1970 period due to growing instability in the financial markets. However, since their emergence, these products have become very popular and by 1990s, they accounted for about two-thirds of total transactions in derivative products.

What is a Mutual Fund?

A Mutual Fund is a body corporate registered with SEBI (Securities Exchange Board of India) that pools money from individuals/corporate investors and invests the same in a variety of different financial instruments or securities such as equity shares, Government securities,

Bonds, debentures etc. Mutual funds can thus be considered as financial intermediaries in the investment business that collect funds from the public and invest on behalf of the investors. Mutual funds issue units to the investors. The appreciation of the portfolio or securities in which the mutual fund has invested the money leads to an appreciation in the value of the units held by investors. The investment objectives outlined by a Mutual Fund in its prospectus are binding on the Mutual Fund scheme. The investment objectives specify the class of securities a Mutual Fund can invest in. Mutual Funds invest in various asset classes like equity, bonds, debentures, commercial paper and government securities. The schemes offered by mutual funds vary from fund to fund. Some are pure equity schemes; others are a mix of equity and bonds. Investors are also given the option of getting dividends, which are declared periodically by the mutual fund, or to participate only in the capital appreciation of the scheme.

What is an Index?

An Index shows how a specified portfolio of share prices is moving in order to give an indication of market trends. It is a basket of securities and the average price movement of the basket of securities indicates the index movement, whether upwards or downwards.

What is a Depository?

A depository is like a bank wherein the deposits are securities (viz. shares, debentures, bonds, government securities, units etc.) in electronic form. What is

Dematerialization? Dematerialization is the process by which physical certificates of an investor are converted to an equivalent number of securities in electronic form and credited to the investor's account with his Depository Participant (DP).

Types Of Stocks

Common and preferred are the two main forms of stock; however, it's also possible for companies to customize different classes of stock in any way they want. The most common reason for this is the company wanting the voting power to remain with a certain group; therefore, different classes of shares are given different voting rights. For example, one class of shares would be held by a select group who are given ten votes per share while a second class would be issued to the majority of investors who are given one vote per share. When there is more than one class of stock, the classes are traditionally designated as Class A and Class B. Berkshire Hathaway (ticker: BRK), has two classes of stock. The different forms are represented by placing the letter behind the ticker symbol in a form like this: "BRKa, BRKb" or "BRK.A, BRK.B".

Common Stock

Common stock is, well, common. When people talk about stocks they are usually referring to this type. In fact, the majority of stock is issued is in this form. We basically went over features of common stock in the last section. Common shares represent ownership in a company and a claim (dividends) on a portion of profits. Investors get one vote per share to elect the board members, who oversee the major decisions made by management.

Over the long term, common stock, by means of capital growth, yields higher returns than almost every other investment. This higher return comes at a cost since common stocks entail the most risk. If a company goes bankrupt and liquidates, the common shareholders will not receive money until the creditors, bondholders and preferred shareholders are paid.

Preferred Stock

Preferred stock represents some degree of ownership in a company but usually doesn't come with the same voting rights. (This may vary depending on the company.) With preferred shares, investors are usually guaranteed a fixed dividend forever. This is different than common stock, which has variable dividends that are never guaranteed. Another advantage is that in the event of liquidation, preferred shareholders are paid off before the common shareholder (but still after debt holders). Preferred stock may also be callable, meaning that the company has the option to purchase the shares from shareholders at any time for any reason (usually for a premium). Some people consider preferred stock to be more like debt than equity. A good way to think of these kinds of shares is to see them as being in between bonds and common shares.

Chapter 4: STOCK MARKET EXCHANGE

Most stocks are traded on exchanges, which are places where buyers and sellers meet and decide on a price. Some exchanges are physical locations where transactions are carried out on a trading floor. You've probably seen pictures of a trading floor, in which traders are wildly throwing their arms up, waving, yelling, and signaling to each other. The other type of exchange is virtually composed of a network of computers where trades are made electronically.

The purpose of a stock market is to facilitate the exchange of securities between buyers and sellers, reducing the risks of investing. Just imagine how difficult it would be to sell shares if you had to call around the neighborhood trying to find a buyer. Really, a stock market is nothing more than a super-sophisticated farmers' market linking buyers and sellers.

Before we go on, we should distinguish between the primary market and the secondary market. The primary market is where securities are created (by means of an IPO) while, in the secondary market, investors trade previously-issued securities without the involvement of the issuing-companies. The secondary market is what people are referring to when they talk about the stock market. It is important to understand that the trading of a company's stock does not directly involve that company.

The New York Stock Exchange

The most prestigious exchange in the world is the New York Stock Exchange (NYSE). The "Big Board" was founded over 200 years ago in 1792 with the signing of the Buttonwood Agreement by 24 New York City stockbrokers and merchants. Currently the NYSE, with stocks like General Electric, McDonald's, Citigroup, Coca-Cola, Gillette and Wal-Mart, is the market of choice for the largest companies in America.

The NYSE is the first type of exchange (as we referred to above), where much of the trading is done face-to-face on a trading floor. This is also referred to as a listed exchange. Orders come in through brokerage firms that are members of the exchange and flow down to floor brokers who go to a specific spot on the floor where the stock trades. At this location, known as the trading post, there is a specific person known as the specialist whose job is to match buyers and sellers. Prices are determined using an auction method: the current price is the highest amount any buyer is willing to pay and the lowest price at which someone is willing to sell. Once a trade has been made, the details are sent back to the brokerage firm, who then notifies the investor who placed the order. Although there is human contact in this process, don't think that the NYSE is still in the Stone Age: computers play a huge role in the process.

The NASDAQ

The second type of exchange is the virtual sort called an over-the-counter (OTC) market, of which the NASDAQ is the most popular. These markets have no central location or floor brokers whatsoever. Trading is done through a computer and telecommunications network of dealers. It used to be that the largest companies were listed only on the NYSE while all other second tier stocks traded on the other exchanges. The tech boom of the late '90s changed all this; now the NASDAQ is home to several big technology companies such as Microsoft, Cisco, Intel, Dell and Oracle. This has resulted in the NASDAQ becoming a serious competitor to the NYSE.

On the NASDAQ brokerages act as market makers for various stocks. A market maker provides continuous bid and ask prices within a prescribed percentage spread for shares for which they are designated to make a market. They may match up buyers and sellers directly but usually they will maintain an inventory of shares to meet demands of investors.

Bombay Stock Exchange (BSE)

BSE is an Indian stock exchange located at Mumbai, Maharashtra, India. It was established in 1875, BSE Ltd. (formerly known as Bombay Stock Exchange Ltd. and established as "The Native Share and Stock Brokers' Association") is one of Asia's fastest stock exchanges, with a speed of 200 microseconds and one of India's leading exchange groups. More than 5,000 companies are listed on BSE, making it the world's top exchange in terms of listed members. The companies listed on BSE Ltd. command a total market capitalization of USD 1.49 trillion as of June 2014.It is also one of the world's top twenty stock exchanges by market capitalization.

National Stock Exchange of India Ltd. (NSE)
NSE is an Indian exchange located at Mumbai, Maharashtra, India. National Stock Exchange (NSE) was established in the mid-1990s as a demutualized electronic exchange. NSE provides a modern, fully automated screen-based trading system, with over two lakh trading terminals, through which investors in every nook and corner of India can trade.

Other Exchanges

The third largest exchange in the U.S. is the American Stock Exchange (AMEX). The AMEX used to be an alternative to the NYSE, but that role has since been filled by the NASDAQ. In fact, the National Association of Securities Dealers (NASD), which is the parent of NASDAQ, bought the AMEX in 1998. Almost all trading now on the AMEX is in small-cap stocks and derivatives.

There are many stock exchanges located in just about every country around the world. American markets are undoubtedly the largest, but they still represent only a fraction of total investment around the globe. The two other main financial hubs are London, home of the London Stock Exchange, and Hong Kong, home of the Hong Kong Stock Exchange. The last place worth mentioning is the over-the-counter bulletin board (OTCBB). The NASDAQ is an over-the-counter market, but the term commonly refers to small public companies that don't meet the listing requirements of any of the regulated markets, including the NASDAQ. The OTCBB is home to penny stocks because there is little to no regulation. This makes investing in an OTCBB stock very risky.

Chapter 5:
THE BULLS, THE BEARS AND THE FARM

The bulls and bears are in a constant struggle. If you haven't heard of these terms already, you undoubtedly will as you begin to invest.

The Bulls

A bull market is when everything in the economy is great, people are finding jobs, gross domestic product (GDP) is growing, and stocks are rising. Things are just plain rosy! Picking stocks during a bull market is easier because everything is going up. Bull markets cannot last forever though, and sometimes they can lead to dangerous situations if stocks become overvalued. If a person is optimistic and believes that stocks will go up, he or she is called a "bull" and is said to have a "bullish outlook".

The Bears

A bear market is when the economy is bad, recession is looming and stock prices are falling. Bear markets make it tough for investors to pick profitable stocks. One solution to this is to make money when stocks are falling using a technique called short selling. Another strategy is to wait on the sidelines until you feel that the bear market is nearing its end, only starting to buy in anticipation of a bull market. If a person is pessimistic, believing that stocks are going to drop, he or she is called a "bear" and said to have a "bearish outlook"

The Other Animals on the Farm - Chickens and Pigs

Chickens are afraid to lose anything. Their fear overrides their need to make profits and so they turn only to money-market securities or get out of the markets entirely. While it's true that you should never invest in something over which you lose sleep, you are also guaranteed never to see any return if you avoid the market completely and never take any risk,

Pigs are high-risk investors looking for the one big score in a short period of time. Pigs buy on hot tips and invest in companies without doing their due diligence. They get impatient, greedy, and emotional about their investments, and they are drawn to high-risk securities without putting in the proper time or money to learn about these investment vehicles. Professional traders love the pigs, as it's often from their losses that the bulls and bears reap their profits.

What Type of Investor Will You Be?

There are plenty of different investment styles and strategies out there. Even though the bulls and bears are constantly at odds, they can both make money with the changing cycles in the market. Even the chickens see some returns, though not a lot. The one loser in this picture is the pig.

Make sure you don't get into the market before you are ready. Be conservative and never invest in anything you do not understand. Before you jump in without the right knowledge, think about this old stock market saying:

"Bulls make money, bears make money, but pigs just get slaughtered!"

Chapter 6:
THE ABC OF STOCK MARKET JARGON

Have you ever opened up the business section of a newspaper and wondered – what in Wall Street's name *are they talking about?* The all-too-common use of stock market jargon – words and phrases only insiders use – has made investing seem overwhelming and confusing. Just like trying to understand a teenage girl, if you're not *"down with the lingo"*, you're in big trouble.

Wall Street stock market jargon has the potential to be even more damaging; **it promotes confusion,** which leads to apathy, which leads to you not paying enough attention to the markets and your money.

Here is some of the more common headache-inducing stock market jargon explained:

(a) "The market is up 100 points today"

When someone talks about the "the market", they're

not talking about *all* 6,000+ stocks on the exchanges.

The "market" is actually represented by the 500 biggest names on the exchanges, on a list known as the S&P 500. This list of stocks is called an **index**, and since it represents the market, it is known as a *market* index.

The points refer to the *price* of the index. Each unit is a point. So, if the S&P 500 is at 1,200, that means it is at 1,200 points. If the S&P climbs from 1,200 to 1,300, you will hear that the "the market is up 100 points today". So now you know!

(b) "The market is crashing" or "The market is rallying"

These two statements are the opposite of each other, but both are used frequently. When you hear that the market is crashing, it doesn't mean that the sky is falling – it merely means that people are selling off their **stocks**. In a crash, people sell their stocks rapidly fearing that a bear market (see above) is coming. Because everyone sells off their stocks quickly, prices drop, causing a "crash".

But markets swing, and unlike gravity, *what goes down usually comes up*. As investors feel the market turn (read: bull market), **they start buying stocks again**. The rapid buying causes stock prices to climb. The climb back up is also known as *rallying*.

(c) Market Timing

What is Market Timing? Obviously, it has to do with both time and the market, but what else? It is actually a trading strategy that attempts to buy and sell stocks by (trying to) predict what their future prices will be. You've heard of *buy low, sell high* - a market timer tries to buy when the market is at it's lowest point, and sell when it's at its highest.

(d) A "Tick"

No, we don't mean the problem that you might be having with your dog or cat. **A tick represents the movement in a stock's price.** The reason it's called a tick is because in the old days, stock market data used to come through **a "ticker" machine** that punched holes in paper to represent the price, and made a "ticking" noise. Confusing? Don't worry – they ditched that practice long ago. Basically, a price lower than the previous price is known as a *down-tick,* and a price higher is known as an *up-tick*.

(e) Double-Dip

Double-Dips don't *only* refer to the hilarious party foul. It refers to an economy heading back into a recession just as it has begun recovering from one. A recession following a recession without at least 6 months of a proper recovery (and since we'd be hypocrites to use jargon in a demystification article – **a recession is an extended down period in the economy**).

(f) Paper-Trading

Paper-trading refers to trading with fake or play money. In fact, Wallstreetsurvivor.com is an example of a paper-trading system! As a beginner, paper-trading allows you to build the confidence to test out the stock market for both basic trades as well as those potentially million dollar ones. Either way, it is a good idea to paper trade before risking your hard-earned money in the markets.

(g) "Quantitative Easing will bolster the economy"

Fancy words. But you could easily rephrase this sentence to read "Governments create and dump new money into the financial markets to push them up." It inadvertently increases stock market activity while providing more money for people to spend. But, keep in mind, this solution is like a band-aid. It is temporary, so don't get too carried away thinking that everything is back to normal.

(h) "Analysts raise outlook for company"

Analysts are great with their predictions…*when they're right, that is*. Financial Analysts are people that work in financial companies, **whose sole job is to find out everything they can about a company, and to make buy/sell recommendations to investors.** So when analysts raise their outlook for a company, they expect the company to make more money than expected. If they are right, they are paid very well. *If they are wrong, they are paid very well.*

Be careful and do your own research into the stock. Do not make trades based solely on analyst expectations. Why? Analysts often have to give a buy or sell recommendation on a company that is paying them for other services. Which recommendation would you choose if you were them?

Remember…

This is just a bit of the financial jargon out there. The trick is not to get intimidated by it, but rather to call it out and simplify it. Ask someone if you can't figure it out yourself. The only way to make money in the stock market is by understanding what you are dealing with. Jargon might sound cool, but if not understood, can be very costly.

Chapter 7:
HOW TO READ A STOCK TABLE/QUOTE

Any financial paper has stock quotes that will look something like the image below:

52W high	52W low	Stock	Ticker	Div	Yield %	P/E	Vol 00s	High	Low	Close	Net chg
s45.39	19.75	ResMed	RMD			52.5	3831	42.00	39.51	41.50	-1.90
11.63	3.55	Revlon A	REV				162	6.09	5.90	6.09	+0.12
77.25	55.13	RioTinto	RTP	2.30	3.2		168	72.75	71.84	72.74	+0.03
31.31	16.63	RitchieBr	RBA			20.9	15	24.49	24.29	24.49	-0.01
8.44	1.75	RiteAid	RAD				31028	4.50	4.20	4.31	+0.21
s38.63	18.81	RobtHalf	RHI			26.5	6517	27.15	26.50	26.50	+0.14
51.25	27.69	Rockwell	ROK	1.02	2.1	14.5	6412	47.99	47.00	47.54	+0.24

Column 1 · Column 2 · Column 3 · Column 4 · Column 5 · Column 6 · Column 7 · Column 8 · Column 9 · Column 10 · Column 11 · Column 12

Columns 1 & 2: 52-Week High and Low - These are the highest and lowest prices at which a stock has traded over the previous 52 weeks (one year). This typically does not include the previous day's trading.

Column 3: Company Name & Type of Stock - This

column lists the name of the company. If there are no special symbols or letters following the name, it is common. Different symbols imply different classes of shares. For example, "pf" means the shares are preferred stock.

Column 4: Ticker Symbol - This is the unique alphabetic name which identifies the stock. If you watch financial TV, you have seen the ticker tape move across the screen, quoting the latest prices alongside this symbol. If you are looking for stock quotes online, you always search for a company by the ticker symbol. If you don't know what a particular company's ticker is you can search for it at:http://finance.yahoo.com/l.

Column 5: Dividend Per Share - This indicates the annual dividend payment per share. If this space is blank, the company does not currently pay out dividends.

Column 6: Dividend Yield - The percentage return on the dividend. Calculated as annual dividends per share divided by price per share.

Column 7: Price/Earnings Ratio -This is calculated by dividing the current stock price by earnings per share from the last four quarters. For more detail on how to interpret this, see our P/E Ratio tutorial.

Column 8: Trading Volume - This figure shows the total number of shares traded for the day, listed in hundreds. To get the actual number traded, add "00" to the end of the number listed.

Column 9 & 10: Day High and Low - This indicates

the price range at which the stock has traded at throughout the day. In other words, these are the maximum and the minimum prices that people have paid for the stock.

Column 11: Close - The close is the last trading price recorded when the market closed on the day. If the closing price is up or down more than 5% than the previous day's close, the entire listing for that stock is bold-faced. Keep in mind, you are not guaranteed to get this price if you buy the stock the next day because the price is constantly changing (even after the exchange is closed for the day). The close is merely an indicator of past performance and except in extreme circumstances serves as a ballpark of what you should expect to pay.

Column 12: Net Change - This is the dollar value change in the stock price from the previous day's closing price. When you hear about a stock being "up for the day," it means the net change was positive.

Quotes on the Internet

Nowadays, it's far more convenient for most to get stock quotes off the Internet. This method is superior because most sites update throughout the day and give you more information, news, charting, research, etc.

To get quotes, simply enter the ticker symbol into the quote box of any major financial site like *Yahoo! Finance*, CBS *Marketwatch*, or *MSN Moneycentral*. The example below shows a quote for Microsoft (MSFT) from Yahoo Finance. Interpreting the data is exactly the same as with the newspaper.

Chapter 8:
STOCK MARKET FORECASTING

Market forecasting is a challenging part of stock market analysis as market prediction has become the most complex task of an analyst. Market forecasting helps a trader to choose the type of security, the time to buy or sell a security and the amount that they should invest on that security.

The type of analysis used by the traders or market analysts falls into two major categories-
1. Fundamental Analysis
2. Technical Analysis

Both of the above methods rely on certain information that comes from various news sources, analytical data or investments charts.

Fundamental Analysis

Fundamental analysis involves careful study of company's financial operations, economic condition, assets, debts, management, products and completion. Thus fundamental analysis is based on the study of financial and industry information of a company to predict the movement of the price of its stock. Fundamental analysis is usually helpful in long term investment and day traders do not rely much on it. However some believe that the simultaneous study of fundamentals and technical can result better for day trading.

Technical Analysis

Technical analysis is the method of evacuating securities by analyzing stock charts. It includes the analysis of market data, volume and open interest in order to predict the future trend of a stock. The analysts study the company's past performance and study the charts to analyze if there are any patterns in the price of that security. Information about a stock's price, volume and other important information can be displayed on a graphical chart. There are various software where study of such graph can be done very effectively and easily to study the patterns and trends. These patterns further used to determine when to buy or sell a security.

Majority of the day traders rely on technical analysis to make their trading decision. There are many advisories which provide stocks and nifty tips on the basis of technical and fundamental analysis.

Being a beginner, I recommend you to begin investing on the basis of fundamental analysis and for long term. I have explained Fundamental analysis in detail in the next chapter.

Chapter 9:
FUNDAMENTALS FOR INVESTORS

The **stock market** is one of the most important ways for companies to raise money, along with debt markets which are generally more imposing but do not trade publicly. This allows businesses to be publicly traded, and raise additional financial capital for expansion by selling shares of ownership of the company in a public market. The liquidity that an exchange affords the investors enables their holders to quickly and easily sell securities. This is an attractive feature of investing in stocks, compared to other less liquid investments such as property and other immoveable assets. Some companies actively increase liquidity by trading in their own shares.

History has shown that the price of stocks and other

assets is an important part of the dynamics of economic activity, and can influence or be an indicator of social mood. An economy where the stock market is on the rise is considered to be an up-and-coming economy. In fact, the stock market is often considered the primary indicator of a country's economic strength and development.

Stock Analyzing

Investors come in many shapes and forms, so to speak, but there are two basic types. First and most common is the more conservative type, who will choose a stock by viewing and researching the basic value of a company. This belief is based on the assumption that so long as a company is run well and continues turning a profit, the stock price will rise. These investors try to buy growth stocks, those that appear most likely to continue growing for a longer term.

The second but less common type of investor attempts to estimate how the market may behave based purely on the psychology of the market's people and other similar market factors. The second type of investor is more commonly called a "Quant." This investor assumes that the price of a stock will soar as buyers keep bidding back and forth (often regardless of the stock's value), much like an auction. They often take much higher risks with higher potential returns-but with much higher potential for higher losses if they fail.

Fundamentalists

Investors need to consider many factors to find the stock's inherent value. When a stock's price is consistent with its value, it will have reached the target goal of an "efficient" market. The efficient market theory states that stocks are always correctly priced since everything publicly known about the stock is reflected in its market price. This theory also implies that analyzing stocks is pointless since all information known is currently reflected in the current price. To put it simply:

- The stock market sets the prices.
- Analysts weigh known information about a company and thereby determine value.
- The price does not have to equal the value. The efficient market theory is as the name implies a theory. If it were law, prices would instantly adapt to information as it became available. Since it is a theory instead of law, this is not the case. Stock prices move above and below company values for both rational and irrational reasons.

Fundamental Analysis endeavors to ascertain the future value of a stock by means of analyzing current and/or past financial strength of a particular company. Analysts attempt to determine if the stock price is above or below value and what that means to the future of that stock. There are a multitude of factors used for this purpose. Basic terminology that helps the investor understand the analysts determination include:

- **"Value Stocks"** are those that are below market

value, and include the bargain stocks listed at 50 cents per dollar of value.

- **"Growth Stocks"** are those with earnings growth as the primary consideration.
- **"Income Stocks"** are investments providing a steady income source. This is primarily through dividends, but bonds are also common investment tools used to generate income.
- **"Momentum Stocks"** are growth companies currently coming into the market picture. Their share prices are increasing rapidly.

To make sound <u>fundamental decisions</u>, all of the following factors must be considered. The previous terminology will be the underlying determining factor in how each will be used, based upon investor bias.

1. Earnings: As usual, the earnings of a particular company are the main deciding factor. Company earnings are the profits after taxes and expenses. The stock and bond markets are mainly driven by two powerful dynamisms: earnings and interest rates. Harsh competition often accompanies the flow of money into these markets, moving into bonds when interest rates go up and into stocks when earnings go up. More than any other factor, a company's earnings create value, although other admonitions must be considered with this idea.

2. EPS (Earnings Per Share) is defined as the amount of reported income, per share, that the company has on hand at any given time to pay dividends to common stockholders or to reinvest in itself. This indicator of a company's condition is a very powerful way to forecast the future of a stock's price. Earnings Per Share is arguably one of the most widely used fundamental ratios.

3. P/E (price/earnings) Ratio: Fair price of a stock is also determined by the P/E (price/earnings) ratio. For example, if a particular company's stock is trading at $60 and its EPS is $6 per share, it has a P/E of 10, meaning that investors can expect a 10% cash flow return.

Equation: $6/$60 = 1/10 = 1/(PE) = 0.10 = 10%

Along these same lines, if it's making $3 a share, it has a multiple of 20. In this case, an investor may receive a 5% return, as long as current conditions remain the same in the future.

Example: $3/$60 = 1/20 = 1/(P/E) = 0.05 = 5%

Certain industries have different P/E ratios. For instance, banks have low P/E's, normally in the range of 5 to 12. High tech companies have higher P/E ratios on the other hand, generally around 15 to 30. On the other hand, in the not too distance past, triple-digit P/E ratios for internet-stocks were seen. These were stocks with no earnings but high P/E ratios, defying market efficiency theories.

A low P/E is not a true indication of exact value. Price volatility, range, direction, and noteworthy news regarding the stock must be considered first. The investor must also consider why any given P/E is low. P/E is best used to compare industry-similar companies.

The Beardstown Ladies suggests that any P/E lower than 5 and/or above 35 be examined closely for errors, since the market average is between 5 and 20 historically.

Peter Lynch suggests a comparison of the P/E ratio with the company growth rate. Lynch considers the stock fairly priced only if they are about equal. If it is less than the growth rate, it could be a stock bargain. To put it into perspective, the basic belief is that a P/E ratio half the growth rate is very positive, and one that is twice the growth rate is very negative.

Other studies suggest that a stock's P/E ratio has little effect on the decision to buy or sell stock (William J. O'Neal, founder of the Investor's Business Daily, in his studies of successful stock moves). He says the stock's current earnings record and annual earnings increases, however, are vital.

It is necessary to mention that the value as represented by the P/E and/or Earnings per Share are useless to investors prior to stock purchase. Money is made after stock is bought, not before. Therefore, it is the future that will pay, both in dividends and growth. This means that investors need to pay as much attention to future earnings estimates as to the historical record.

4. Basic PSR (Price/Sales Ratio) is similar to P/E ratio, except that the stock price is divided by sales per share as opposed to earnings per share.

- For many analysts, the PSR is a better value indicator than the P/E. This is because earnings often fluctuate wildly, while sales tend to follow more dependable trends.
- PSR may be also be a more accurate measure of value because sales are more difficult to manipulate than earnings. The credibility of financial institutions have suffered through the Enron/Global Crossing/WorldCom, et al, debacle, and investors have learned how manipulation does go on within large financial institutions.
- The PSR by itself is not very effective. It is effectively used only in conjunction with other measures. James O'Shaughnessy, in his book What Works on Wall Street, found that, when the PSR is used with a measure of relative strength, it becomes "the King of value factors."

5. Debt Ratio shows the percentage of debt a company has as compared to shareholder equity. In other words, how much a company's operation is being financed by debt.
- Remember, under 30% is positive, over 50% is negative.
- A successful operation with ascending profitability and a well marketed product can be destroyed by the company's debt load, because the earnings are sacrificed to offset the debt.

6. ROE (Equity Returns) is found by dividing net income (after taxes) by the owner's equity.

- ROE is often considered to be the most important financial ratio (for stockholders) and the best measure of a company's management abilities. ROE gives stockholders the confidence they need to know that their money is well-managed.
- ROE should always increase on a yearly basis.

7. Price/Book Value Ratio (a.k.a. Market/Book Ratio) compares the market price to the stock's book value per share. This ratio relates what the investors believe a company (stock) is worth to what that company's accountants say it is worth per recognized accounting principles. For example, a low ratio would suggest that the investors believe that the company's assets have been overvalued based on its financial statements.

While investors would like the stocks to be trading at the same point as book value, in reality, most stocks trade either at a value above book value or at a discount.

Stocks trading at 1.5 to 2 times book value are about the limit when searching for value stocks. Growth stocks justify higher ratios, because they grant the anticipation of higher earnings. The ideal would be stocks below book value, at wholesale prices, but this rarely happens. Companies with low book value are often targets of a takeover, and are normally avoided by investors (at least until the takeover is complete and the process begins anew).

Book value was more important in a time when most industrial companies had actual hard assets, such as factories, to back up their stock. Sadly, the value of this measure has waned as companies with low capital have become commercial giants (i.e. Microsoft). Videlicet, look for low book value to keep the data in perspective.

8. Beta compares the volatility of the stock to that of the market. A beta of 1 proposes that a stock price moves up and down at the same rate as the market overall. A beta of 2 means that when the market drops the stock is likely to move double that amount. A beta of 0 means it does not move at all. A negative Beta means it moves in the opposite direction of the market, spelling a loss for the investor.

9. Capitalization is the total value of all of a company's outstanding shares, and is calculated by multiplying the market price per share by the total number of outstanding shares.

10. Institutional Ownership refers to the percent of a company's outstanding shares that are owned by institutions, mutual funds, insurance companies, etc., which move in and out of positions in very large blocks. Some institutional ownership can actually provide a measure of stability and make contributions to the roll with their buying and selling, respectively. Investors consider this an important factor because they can make use of the extensive research done by these institutions before making their own portfolio decisions. The importance of institutions in market action cannot be overstated, and accounts for over 70% of the dollar volume traded daily.

Market efficiency is a marketplace goal at all times. Anyone who puts money into a stock would like to see a return on their investment. Nevertheless, as before-mentioned, human emotions will always drive the market, causing over- and undervalue of common stocks. Investors must take advantage of patterns using modern computing tools to find the stocks most undervalued as well as develop the correct response to these market patterns, such as rolling within a channel (recognizing trends) with intelligence.

Chapter 10:
WHAT CAUSES STOCK PRICES TO CHANGE?

The stock market is extremely complicated - all the more reason to jump in with your eyes closed. (Just kidding...) There are many aspects to the stock market that must be reasonably taking into account before investing, from buying and selling stocks, to stock market pricing.

Consumers often have some idea about how the stock market generally works, but few understand the mechanics of stock prices.

Complexity of the Process

Admittedly, it is tough to understand how the prices of stocks are set, as this is not something commonly addressed in typical discussions of stock market concepts. Many wonder pause to ask what causes the more popular and successful stocks to trade for a low price, and why many unknown stocks are available for prices that seem extremely high. There are actually a number of factors that determine this.

High Investor Confidence Raises Price

Investor confidence in a company is one of the major determinants of the trading price of a stock. The level of comfort and positive anticipation investors have is largely based on actual performance - or even mere perceptions - about the future of the company and the value of its stock.

Shareholders receive quarterly financial reports covering the company's performance. This financial information includes details on the company's expenditures, sales, and earnings for that quarter.

Though such hard financial data is useful, it is not the only predictor of performance. Oftentimes shareholders make decisions based simply on what they believe will happen in the future, even if that belief is not centered on the company itself.

Decisions Made Based on Perceptions

The impacts of perceptions about the stock market are significant. They can actually sway the investing behaviors of stockholders more so than detailed financial reports and hard data. The opinions of economists and commentators about the company or even the financial world in general have a heavy influence on the price of stock.

If there are abundant positive rumors going around

about the company's performance, it is likely investors will lean toward purchasing stock from the company.

However, when there's bad news in the air (pending war across the ocean, high unemployment reports, inflation rising, etc.), people tend to sell a lot more stock, driving the price down.

Supply/Demand of Stock

The higher the demand for a stock, the greater the tendency for prices to rise. Conversely, the trend for prices of stocks with a large supply of shares is typically to fall.

Apprehension (from real people) about different kinds of stocks and the hard data itself collectively determine the worth of stocks.

<u>The important things to grasp about this subject are the following:</u>
1. At the most fundamental level, supply and demand in the market determines stock price.

2. Price times the number of shares outstanding (market capitalization) is the value of a company. Comparing just the share price of two companies is meaningless.

3. Theoretically, earnings are what affect investors' valuation of a company, but there are other indicators that investors use to predict stock price. Remember, it is investors' sentiments, attitudes and expectations that ultimately affect stock prices.

4. There are many theories that try to explain the way stock prices move the way they do. Unfortunately, there is no one theory that can explain everything.

Chapter 11:
HOW TO FIND GOOD STOCKS - 3 PROVEN STEPS

You may be asking yourself lately how to find good stocks?

Traditional bellwether companies have recently fallen on tough times. Several have missed earnings estimates while others have cut their long standing dividends. In some severe cases, a few of these companies have even declared bankruptcy. What is a long term investor to do?

In the past, smart investors understood that financially stable dividend producing stocks were a value. They would build a diversified portfolio around these securities. Many invested in these types of stocks as part of their retirement savings. Unfortunately, many of these same investors have seen any returns wiped out along with any plans on early retirement.

While there are several companies who have seen their share prices come crashing down, there are still some really great companies out there which would make good investments. Here are 3 proven methods to use so that you can figure out how to find good stocks.

Dividend Stocks

Identifying companies that consistently raise their dividends is a good list to start from. Be careful not to solely choose a stock just because they have a history of raising their dividends. You must first complete additional due diligence to make sure a company's current financial state warrants continued performance.

Long Term Growth

Run a stock screen looking for companies with projected long term growth that exceeds its peers. Standout companies should have optimistic long term growth projections to warrant a purchase. Keep in mind not to use this screen as your only basis for making a purchase.

Financial Statements

If you want to know how to find good stocks, another option is to look at financial statements. Keep track of a company's quarterly financial statements and pay attention to the fine details. Several times potential red flags can be identified in these statements. You should also make it a good practice to listen to the quarterly investor conference calls to pick up good tips.

Stock investing does not have to be a difficult task.

While the market has seen historical volatility and declining share prices, there is always a place to invest your money. Using a collection of the proven methods above can put you well on your way to identifying how to find good stocks! Combining several due diligent steps in your stock selection is key to your success and if you will make money or not.

Do you know which ones to avoid?

When looking for good stocks to buy using a longer term value investing approach, I am immediately confronted with the multitude of companies listed on my stock market. I manage the task of how to buy good stocks by narrowing the field of companies to those that appear to provide the greatest value with the least risk.

If I can rule out a substantial number of riskier companies for good reasons, it helps to reduce the complexity of the task. Listed below are classes of companies I generally rule out for the reasons outlined. By eliminating these companies, I will be more likely to minimize risk when choosing from the remaining companies.

Initial Public Offerings (IPOs)-

These are companies who offer stock to the public for the first time by applying to list them on a stock market at a listing price via a prospectus - a document providing essential details about the company. I generally avoid this class of investment.

IPOs, or initial public offerings, are often issued by smaller, younger companies seeking additional capital to expand, but can also involve larger privately owned companies looking to go public.

IPOs can be a risky investment as it is difficult to predict what the stock will do on its first day of trading, and from then on. There is often little historical data to go on in order to analyze the company. The directors set the listing price that the investor has to pay. You can be sure that they will set the price at a level that will ensure a good profit for them.

But will you make a profit? Don't bet on it unless you can be confident that there is a large pool of punters hoping that they can make a profit too, and are sufficiently enthusiastic that they drive the price up from the listing price.

Single Resource Companies

These are companies that usually explore and develop mineral or oil resources. Companies that mine or explore for one resource are very dependent on the price that they can sell that resource for, if and when they can market it.

So if you buy into a single resource company, you are taking a bet that the price of that resource will rise. Unless your information sources are better than most, you are in a high risk enterprise. I prefer low risk enterprises!

Capital-Intensive Industries-

They are companies that require large amounts of expensive equipment, machinery or planes in order to trade. Think steel mills, car makers and airline companies for example. Why do I generally avoid them?

Unless the companies continue to inject large amounts of their earnings into new equipment, they will lose their competitive edge, and one way or other earnings will be lost to shareholders.

Penny Stocks or Small-Cap Stocks

These stocks are usually defined by their share price. The price you are talking about depends on the size of the particular country or stock market. For example- Those stock that sell for less than $5 in the USA or less than $1 in Australia.

Why do I avoid them? Mainly because they tend to exhibit either low liquidity (a low trading volume) and you may not be able to sell them when you want to - or high volatility (the price jumps around a lot) - or both!

Regulated Markets and Price-Competitive Companies

I avoid companies that operate in regulated markets where possible, as they are always at the whim of the regulating authority (commonly government bodies). They are in a no-win situation because if they are successful in making a decent profit, the regulator usually doesn't like the idea - and you guessed it, moves to tighten the regulations!

Price-competitive companies have a different problem. They have to be the cheapest business in their industry and usually don't have an economic moat to protect them. They always have their competitors biting at their heels. Unless they can achieve large scale and can make it very expensive for others to enter the market, they are continually under threat.

In Summary, the benefit to me in excluding the above categories of companies from consideration of good stocks to buy is that the overall risk in choosing to invest in some of the remaining companies will be significantly reduced.

Risk reduction, while maintaining a high return, is the name of the game! The risk of loss is real - it can be minimized but not eliminated.

Chapter 12: POWER OF DIVERSIFICATION

Are you looking to make and save enough cash for your retirement in the near future? Do you have money idly waiting in your desk drawer? Do you feel that bank rates are just too low to get a significant return on investment per year? Why not try something that is riskier, and at the same time, will give you higher returns? I am not talking about simple stock market trading. What I am talking about is using the diversification strategy in stock market trading. It is not as complicated as you may think.

What is Diversification?

It is a risk management technique that mixes a wide

variety of investments within a portfolio. It is designed to minimize the impact of any one security on overall portfolio performance. Diversification is possibly the best way to reduce the risk in a portfolio.

What is a Portfolio?

A Portfolio is a combination of different investment assets mixed and matched for the purpose of achieving an investor's goal(s). Items that are considered a part of your portfolio can include any asset you own-from shares, debentures, bonds, mutual fund units to items such as gold, art and even real estate etc. However, for most investors a portfolio has come to signify an investment in financial instruments like shares, debentures, fixed deposits, mutual fund units.

Now, before I start discussing the diversified strategy for stock trading, here's a saying that I would like you guys to keep in mind.

"Don't put all your eggs in one basket".

This strategy entails investing in different kinds of stocks that do not move together perfectly in the fluctuations of the stock market. Thus, you get a diversified portfolio. When I say, "stocks that do not move together", I mean that the stocks that you should be investing in are stocks that both are rise in price in economic booms and in recessions. These stocks should be in different sizes and from many different industries.

You would probably tell me,

So that would mean that, even in normal markets or economic booms, you should also invest in stocks that are relatively low during these times. Why? Are you crazy?

These stocks serve as a buffer so that when recession strikes, just like what happened a couple of months ago, you won't lose everything. By having a diversified portfolio, you decrease the variability of your stock and thus reduce risk.

Two Types of Risk

There are actually two types of risk when it comes to trading in the stock market. The first one is the market risk and the second one is diversifiable risk.

1. The Market Risk is the risk that is common to all of the firms. Such risks are recessions, when cost of goods rise, etc. This is the kind of risk that cannot be diversified away even if you have diversified portfolios.

2. The Diversifiable Risk is the risk that is unique to every firm. These risks include labor strikes, bankruptcy, the manager running away with the company's money etc. This kind of risk can be diversified away when one has a diversified portfolio.

Some Benefits of having Diversified Portfolio

A good investment portfolio is a mix of a wide range of asset class. Different securities perform differently at any point in time, so with a mix of asset types, your entire portfolio does not suffer the impact of a decline of any one security. When your stocks go down, you may still have the stability of the bonds in your portfolio. There have been all sorts of academic studies and formulas that demonstrate why diversification is important, but it's really just the simple practice of "not putting all your eggs in one basket." If you spread your investments across various types of assets and markets, you'll reduce the risk of your entire portfolio getting affected by the adverse returns of any single asset class.

1. Less Risk! That is the best benefit I could think of. The more stocks in your portfolio, the more risk that is diversified away.

2. Assures you that even with the fluctuation in the stock market prices, your portfolio is more secure than if you are only investing in one particular stock. You are given more assurance that you are not wasting your money or are not throwing it all away.

Why Diversification Is So Important?

You should never trust just one stock so much that you are willing to risk all you money in it and no other stock. A wise investor always spreads out their money among several different stocks so as to minimize the effect of a bad day in the stock market. It doesn't matter how how or how stable you think a company is, the fact is you should never invest solely in that company.

We are not just talking about buying different stocks here. We are also talking about investing in different industries. If oil is doing badly then commodities may be doing well or vice versa. Just concentrate on investing in several different areas so your portfolio is affected by a big hit in one specific industry.

It's certainly been proven that investors with diversified portfolios see a more consistent return that investors who invest in only one or two stocks. Diversification is also a great way to decrease risk while maintaining aggressive returns. You can even diversify with penny stocks.

Let's say you invested in this one hot stock that you were completely sure about. One day that company has some bad news and investors make run for it and the stocks takes a dive. That's bad news for your poor portfolio. Let's say that on the other hand you invested in 10 different stocks. One of those stocks has a bad day but you aren't so worried about it because you have nine other stocks keeping your portfolio strong. See the difference?

You don't have to limit your portfolio to stocks. You can also invest in real estate, real property, and bank CDs just to name a few. The whole idea of diversification is to protect yourself while making satisfying gains. So around and study out the best investment options for your particular goals. Diversify along the way to win the game.

To demonstrate a real world case of how important diversification is I will tell you a personal story. When I first started investing I put 10k down on a very popular stock that did nothing but climb in value year after year. I simply had no reason to believe that this stock would perform in any other way except a positive direction. Wrong!! I lost 5k as a sadly watched this stock plummet as the result of corporate fraud. Lesson learned. Diversify!! That was a lesson learned the hard way for me but you don't have to learn the hard way. Take it from me. Invest in more than one good stock, at least 5.

Chapter 13:
READY TO BEGIN INVESTING?

If you're ready to jump into stock investing, don't make the mistake of just hiring someone to manage your accounts. Managing your own stocks, even as a beginner investor, is a relatively simple process and there are several things you can do to increase your chances of success with trading. Kicking off an investment strategy as early as possible can help you learn from your mistakes without losing too much right off the bat, but there are still a number of mistakes to avoid as you move forward. Here are just five important stock investing tips for beginners:

1. Learn as much as possible about different stocks. Gauge the performance of different stocks you are interested in and do some research on various

companies. How long has the company been trading? What are the share price trends? When was the latest increase or decrease? Doing your homework can help you make more informed decisions about your stock trading strategy.

2. Understand the different levels of risk. Some investments are much riskier than others, but the higher the risk, the higher the return. Ask yourself what type of risk you are truly comfortable with and if you want to invest in both low-risk and high-risk investments. This strategy is usually a good idea as a beginner, because you'll be able to gauge how comfortable you are with each type of account.

3. Set up a savings account just for investments. Don't make the mistake of investing all of your life savings in the stock market. You need to make sure you still have a savings cushion for yourself, in the event that you do end up losing your funds in the markets. Set up a secondary savings account that is just for investment and treat it like a completely separate savings account. Continue contributing to this account as you move forward and keep track of its growth as part of your financial management strategy.

4. Check prices of stocks before you trade. It's easier than ever to find out the current prices of stocks online. Use tools such as Google Finance or Yahoo! Finance to track down the latest prices and find out more information about each stock and company. Review the current price and average price before you start trading.

5. Keep track of your investments. Get things

organized so that you can keep track of how well your investments are performing, and whether you are seeing some positive growth. You don't need to check these daily, but checking your portfolio and accounts at least once per month or once every two months can make it easier to see the value of your trading efforts. You'll need to retrieve current prices each time you check your accounts, and populate the data into a worksheet or spreadsheet to get an accurate value for your portfolio.

Stock investing can be tricky for beginners, but there are several things you can do to increase your chances of success with the stock market. Use these tips to start your investing strategy on the right foot.

Chapter 14: COMMON MISTAKES THAT NEWBIES MAKE

Before you start investing in stock market, remember that you cannot become rich overnight. At the same time, if you do your research properly and plan your investments, you can definitely make some good money. But, there are some common mistakes committed by investors like you and these mistakes may land you in deep trouble. Try to avoid them and safeguard yourself from such troubles.

Mistake #1: Thinking that speed is important. We believe that we could actually compete against other investors and that the fastest investor will win the race. We therefore make frantic trades on every little bit of market information or rumor. In reality of course, there is no way we can compete with the large professional traders who have vast resources at their disposal. Never put yourself in a position where your success hinges around speed and timing.

Mistake #2: Thinking that foresight is as accurate as hindsight. For all of us hindsight is a perfect 20/20 because the event has already occurred. Because hindsight is easy, we are tempted to believe that our foresight is as good and we come to rely on it implicitly. A little common sense should tell you that this attitude is asking for trouble.

Mistake #3: Letting success stories mislead you. For every one lottery winner, there are millions of losers. This is called confirmation error and wishful thinking leads us to believe that our lucky number is going to win. And we try and use evidence or even dreams to support this conviction. It is exactly the same for stock trading. Rational investors realize that events are essentially random in nature and trade accordingly.

Mistake # 4: Getting carried away by greed or fear. Stock markets are no different from any other financial markets where the governing emotions are greed and fear. Since investors, even large institutional ones, are driven by a herd instinct, they stampede into markets out of greed and stampede out of markets driven by fear. Use your judgment and your common sense to avoid being overly influenced by these emotions.

Mistake #5: Expecting to get rich overnight. Stock

trading, like any form of investment, is all about risk management. If you are averse to risk, the stock market is not the place for you and you should seek relatively safe investments such as banks or securities. You should be a long-term investor and set goals for yourself accordingly though there will be spells (sometimes prolonged) when you are in a losing position. You should also diversify your bets instead of risking everything on a single wager. If you attempt to become a millionaire overnight, you will find yourself in an unacceptable high risk situation which is a surefire recipe from losing your shirt.

Mistake#6: Never sell your stocks when there is a panic selling in the stock market. Panic selling is mostly triggered by rumors only. It is better to stay invested even when there is a panic selling going on in the market. The market will definitely bounce back after this trend is over. You should wait for it to sell your stocks so that you can have some decent returns.

Mistake#7: Too much spreading of stocks should also be avoided. Diversification is good to a certain extent but it should not be over-done. You may also find it difficult to manage your portfolio if your investment is spread over a number of stocks. Further, if your total investment is small, each of your stock will be too small to fetch you sizable returns.

Mistake#8: Avoid being excessively confident about your own analysis. Overconfidence may lead to excessive investment and this may prove to be dangerous. Put a stop-loss order on every "buy". This will limit your losses if something goes wrong and the stock-value declines instead of appreciating. Likewise, refrain from being excessively dependent upon the findings of analysts. Even analysts cannot make accurate predictions of stock movements. Of course, it is good to do your research and also listen to the opinions of analysts. But, depending excessively on them is also wrong.

As you can see, the main lesson to be learnt is to be disciplined about your stock trading and not get overly influenced emotions and feelings. Develop your own systems and rules and ensure that your disciplines such as a "stop loss" are followed scrupulously. Don't let yourself be overly influenced by temporary good or bad news and develop long-term goals against which you can monitor your progress. You can then, if necessary, tweak or fine tune your trading system in accordance with market developments.

Chapter 15:
HOW TO BECOME STOCKS GENIUS

Don't be fool - never buy dead stocks

Many investors buy dead stocks with a hope to make money from them. Such thinking is totally absurd. Always remember that the dead stocks have no value and that is why they are dead. However, you could go ahead any buy penny stocks. All dead stocks are penny stocks but not all penny stocks are dead stocks. Many people had tried buying penny stocks and over a period of time they have made millions by investing in such stocks.

Research is the key to success

In stock market trading one has to be really very active while researching for stocks and trading opportunities. The lazier in researching you are, the more money you will lose in the course of your trading. It is very important that a trader must take time to research and find out the best stock for him before he funds in it. If you are also interested in buying the penny stocks and getting rich with them then only hard research could help you buy such stocks. Whatever you do while researching, always remember that it is helping you gaining experience and knowledge of the market. Higher returns in stock trading are only possible if one research deeply.

Always invest in stocks that have good liquidity

Liquidity means the conversion for the share for cash. So, whenever you buy a stock, must check for its liquidity. Of course dead stocks will never provide you liquidity. Shares with more liquidity are popular on the stock markets and of course guarantees you more returns. Checking liquidity of shares is easy. Simply analyze the volume of trades for the past one week of the share you want to check liquidity for. Liquidity refers value of the share and therefore more liquidity means more value and vice versa.

Determine the undervalue stocks and take positions in them

When going for purchasing shares, you must lookout stocks that give you more dividends. This is called as dividend research. So next time you buy the stocks, simply perform dividend research and go for higher dividend paying stocks.

Market watch

Again one of the most crucial task, you need to perform. Before buying any stock, you must look for oversold or overbought stocks and then decide your move. Keeping a watch over the market will help you take good decisions and you will be updated with the current trend of the market.

Effective planning

Before entering the stock trades one must plan his trading strategy effectively. Many investors buy stocks, and do not know when they have to come out of the trade as a result they lose money. If you preplan your trade then not only you will make money but would also be able to avoid emotions (the biggest enemy of a stock trader.)

Check for stocks from reputed companies

This does not means that you have to buy the top stocks that cost very high. By checking for stocks from reputed firms means that before buying stocks of a company you must cross check the reputation of the firm. It will help you determine their trading practices, which indirectly affect value of their stocks. Even if the shares of a company are at low (risk), one could buy invest in them citing the past company performance and its reputation.

Becoming stock market genius is not a tough job. Following few simple tips anybody could become a successful stock market trader.

The stocks, bonds, real estate, foreign currency, mutual funds, certificates of deposit, insurance and savings account are the types of investment that you could use.

Chapter 16:
EXPLORE YOUR STOCKS KNOWLEDGE - QUIZ

1. Companies like their stocks to go up in value because:

(A) They make more money when the stock is at a higher price.

(B) Part of their profits comes from the value of their stock.

(C) The higher the price of their shares, the more likely they are to make higher profits that year

(D) All of the above

(E) None of the above.

2. If you own a share of stock, you:

(A) Own part of the company that issued the stock

(B) Have the right to vote if another company wants to buy the company whose stock you own.

(C) Might receive a check every year that represents your share in the company's profits.
(D) All of the above
(E) None of the above.

3. A stock is to a mutual fund as:
(A) A blind squirrel is to an acorn.
(B) One egg is to a dozen.
(C) A tree is to a forest.
(D) The pitcher is to a baseball team.

4. You are an enterprising high school student. You inherit $10,000 and want to use it to pay for your college education starting in a little over two years. You can't afford to lose money, but you need more for college. Should you:
(A) Invest in the safest blue chip stocks since they will probably be worth a lot more in two years.
(B) Avoid the stock market since two years is too long of a time to invest.
(C) Avoid the stock market since two years is too short of a time to invest.
(D) Find a broker so good he promises to increase your investment by 50% in time for college.

5. You discover your great-great--grandfather named you in his will. The good news is that he left you stock in Coca-Cola. The bad news is that it is only one share he bought in 1919 (ten years before the Great

Depression) for $40. How much is that share worth now?

(A) Nearly 1.8 million dollars.

(B) Barely enough to buy a year's worth of Diet Cherry Coke.

(C) Nearly 7 million dollars.

(D) It has increased a hundredfold and is now worth $4,000.

6. Which of these has the most effect on the price of a stock:

(A) The opinion of investors about the future chances for the company.

(B) The general state of the economy.

(C) The performance of the stock market in general.

(D) How much the company earns in profits

7. You read that the Dow Jones Industrial average has gone down 500 points in the last two weeks. What does this mean to you as an investor:

(A) It's time to sell since prices are headed the wrong direction.

(B) Nothing, since you did not invest in Dow Jones.

(C) Stocks that are part of the average are now cheaper to buy.

(D) Such a major fall in the index indicates serious problems for the economy.

8. The efficient market theory states that:

(A) You can make money in stocks, but are unlikely to "beat the market."

(B) The market is so efficient that only professional stock traders and brokers can make money over the long term. (C) Information about companies is available to everyone so that it is now nearly impossible to actually "make money" in the stock market.

(D) You can make money in stocks but most of that is taken away by broker fees, commissions, and sales charges.

9. If a company listed on the New York Stock Exchange makes a profit it:

(A) Must declare a dividend payable to its shareholders during that year.

(B) Can pay a dividend with the profits or plow the money back into the company to make more profits.

(C) Must pay dividends unless it receives shareholder approval to use the profit for other purposes.

(D) Increases the value of the stock by the amount of the dividend.

(E) Insures that the price of its stock does not drop in value.

10. When you buy a share of stock, the money you pay for it is:

(A) Divided among the stock market, the broker, and the company who issued the stock.

(B) Sent directly to the company in which you invested (after subtracting brokerage fees) for whatever business use it sees fit.

(C) Is sent to the company but how it is used is carefully regulated by the Securities and Exchange Commission.

(D) Goes (after subtracting brokerage fees) to some other person who wants to sell the stock.

So Do You Think You Understand Stocks Quiz?

Answer Key

1. E — None of the above. The price of a stock is what the last person who bought it paid. If the next person to buy a stock pays more, the price goes up. This movement is NOT tied to profits. Companies who earn no profits can see their stock rise while others with profits see their stock price decline. The price of a stock is an opinion about its future.

2. D—All of the above. Companies that sell stock are owned by the shareholders. Shareholders have a right to vote and will receive dividends. Companies do NOT have an obligation to pay dividends.

3. C—A stock is to a mutual fund as a tree is to a forest. B is incorrect because all the eggs are the same while all the shares in the portfolio of a mutual fund are not the same. Plus, if you take one egg away you no

longer have a dozen. D is not correct because you cannot have a baseball game without a pitcher, you can have a mutual fund without a given stock. C is correct since removing a tree still leaves a forest. In fact, a diversity of stocks makes for a healthy fund portfolio just as a diversity of trees makes for a forest more likely to survive.

4. C—Avoid the stock market since two years is too short of a time to invest what must be used in two years to pay for something important. Stock market investing is for long term goals. After two years even a well-planned investment might be worth less.

5. C—Nearly seven million dollars. This question is designed to illustrate the tremendous potential of stocks as a wealth builder. That single share would have split many times and today be 100,000+ shares.

6. A—The opinion of investors about the future chances for the company. The other choices certainly influence stocks, but the value of any given stock is the opinion of investors about its future. The economy can be dreadful, and the company earning no profits at all yet see its stock soar in value.

7. C—Stocks that are part of the average are now cheaper to buy. The Dow Jones average uses a handful of stocks — it is NOT the entire stock market.

8. A—you can make money in stocks, but are unlikely to "beat the market." C is close, but many long term investors do "make money" in stocks.

9. B—can pay a dividend with the profits or plow the money back into the company to make more profits. "Growth stocks" take the latter approach while typically older; "blue chip" stocks take the former. Such a clear distinction is no longer true, but note that although any dividends must be paid to shareholders, there is no obligation to declare dividends.

10. C—Money paid for a stock goes (less broke fees) to a person who agrees to sell the stock. Note that stocks are bought from people who already own them. The only exception is the first offering (Initial Public Offering) used to raise money. Companies do like to see the value of their stock increase, but not because they "make money" on sales at higher prices. Companies make money selling goods or services, not by selling stocks.

Chapter 17: Basic Terminologies

- **NYSE** –The New York Stock Exchange is the largest stock exchange in the world and it's the main one in the US.
- **NASDAQ** - this is the other major stock exchange in the US. Technology companies especially like to use this exchange to be listed on.
- **Stock** - a stock represents part of what you own when you buy a share in a company. The stock market allows you to essentially co-own companies with millions of other owners.
- **Share Price** - this is the price at which a single share in a company is selling for. I can currently buy one share of Google for $475.
- **Stock Broker** - unless you have a Series 7 license and work for a financial institution, you will not be able to buy stocks for yourself. You will need a stock broker, online brokerage account or a financial adviser to make that trade on your

behalf. We'll talk about that in more detail later.
- **Market Cap** - also known as the market capitalization, refers to the size of a company. It's calculated by taking the number of outstanding shares and multiplying that with the share price. The different market cap sizes gives an indication of risk and return potential. A small cap stock has greater potential for high returns, but with a lot more risk than a large cap company.
- **P/E Ratio** - this is the price per earnings ratio. It gives you an indication of how much earnings a company is producing in relation to how much a share of the company costs. Businesses is about making money. This tells you how well a particular company is making money relative to the stock price.
- **Liquidity** - this refers to how liquid or how fast someone can buy or sell a particular stock. If there aren't many shares in a particular stock changing hands on any given day, that means that stock is not liquid. That means if you own that stock, it might be difficult for you to get rid of it.
- **Volatility** - its how much the price of a particular stock or the entire stock market is fluctuating. Volatility is a sign of risky environment. Traders love volatility because they play on the ups and downs to make profits.
- **Volume** - this is how many shares traded in any given time period. You will generally see high volume on days where there is high volatility in the market or when big news about a stock or the economy comes out.
- **Technical Analysis** - since this is a guide to stock market investing for beginners, I won't go

into this in detail. Suffice it to say, this refers to looking at and understanding price chart patterns of a stock.
- **Fundamental Analysis** - this refers to understanding the inherent value of a company and its business. This looks at the company's business lines, revenue sources, financial statements and earnings to see what the value of a company is.

Glossary for Beginners

- **After-hours Deal:**
  The stock market usually closes at 4:00pm. After this scheduled time, deals can also be made but the transaction is dated the next day, known as an after-hours deal.
- **Annual Report:**
  An audit report to shareholders produced yearly. This report is produced by all publicly quoted companies.
- **Balance Sheet:**
  The financial statement which shows the liabilities and assets of a company.
- **Bargain:**
  Regarding sale or purchase in the stock market, bargain is a common word.
- **Bearer Stocks:**
  This is the stock that is unregistered with the owner's name.
- **Bed and Breakfast Deal:**
  This refers to the sale of share and

repurchase on another day. It's done to set up profit or loss for the purpose of tax.
- **Bid Price:**
  This term indicates the sale price of stocks or shares.
- **Blue Button:**
  Refers to the stockbroker's clerk. Only a blue button is allowed on the trading floor.
- **Blue Chip:**
  These are shares of big and reputed companies.
- **Bull:**
  A person who considers the share price of the stock exchange to be on the rise.
- **Call:**
  An extra installment due on shares.
- **Capital:**
  The amount of money used for setting up a new business.
- **Cash Settlement**:
  In the stock exchange, there are certain deals like Gilts which are rendered for cash and not for account settlement. They are settled the next day of the deal.
- **Contract Note**:
  This is a printed confirmation letter from any broker indicating a bargain which is carried out.
- **Coupon**:
  Refers to interest amount payable only for fixed interest stock.
- **Cum Dividend**:
  These are shares that are sold, allowing the

buyer to receive the following dividend.
- **Dawn Raid**:
  Refers to the buying of a huge amount of shares in the morning at the opening of stock market.
- **Dealing**:
  This means the purchase and sale of shares.
- **Debenture:**
  The stock that a company issues which are backed by assets.
- **Depreciation:**
  The amount of money set aside for replacement of the assets.
- **Dividend:**
  The part of the company's profits which is usually distributed to company's shareholders, normally on regular basis.
- **Equities:**
  These are the ordinary shares. They are different from debenture and also from loan stock.
- **Ex-dividend**:
  The share which is bought without any right for receiving the next dividend. This is usually retained by sellers.
- **Final Dividend**:
  This is the dividend which is declared according to the company's annual results.
- **Futures**:
  Contracts that allow any holder the legal right to buy or sell Indexes and Commodities in the future at a price set today.

- **Gross**:
    The interest paid without deducting of tax.
- **Hedge Funds**:
    This means to insure the risk.
- **Initial Public Offering**:
    The issue of new shares by a previously private company as it becomes a public company.
- **Limit Order:**
    This is an order to any stockbroker specifying any fixed price limit.
- **Liquidation:**
    Converting the prevailing assets to cash.
- **Loan Stock:**
    The stock that bears a fixed interest rate. It's different from debenture stock because it's not required to be secured by any asset.
- **Nominee**:
    The term refers to a person acting on the behalf of another in the stock market in documentary as well as financial affairs.
- **Offer Price:**
    Refers to the specific price at which one can buy stocks and shares.
- **Options**: The term means the right to purchase (call option) and sell (put option) a particular share at a particular price within a particular period.
- **Ordinary Share**:
    This is a share where the dividends usually vary in the amount.
- **Over the Counter Market (OTC):**
    Refers to a marketplace outside the main stock market.

- **PLC**:
   This means Public Limited Company (formerly Ltd). In the stock market, some public limited companies are not always quoted.
- **Portfolio**:
   A selection of shares usually held by a person or fund.
- **Proxy**:
   Anybody who votes on another person's behalf if the person is unable to attend a shareholders' meeting.
- **Yearlings**:
   Bonds issued for twelve-month term, mainly by local authorities.
- **Yield:**
   The gross dividend presented as the percentage of the share price.

ALL RIGHTS RESERVED. No part of this publication may be reproduced or transmitted in any form whatsoever, electronic, or mechanical, including photocopying, recording, or by any informational storage or retrieval system without express written, dated and signed permission from the author.

DISCLAIMER AND/OR LEGAL NOTICES: Every effort has been made to accurately represent this book and it's potential. Results vary with every individual, and your results may or may not be different from those depicted. No promises, guarantees or warranties, whether stated or implied, have been made that you will produce any specific result from this book. Your efforts are individual and unique, and may vary from those shown. Your success depends on your efforts, background and motivation.

The material in this publication is provided for educational and informational purposes only and is not intended as medical advice. The information contained in this book should not be used to diagnose or treat any illness, metabolic disorder, disease or health problem. Always consult your physician or health care provider before beginning any nutrition or exercise program. Use of the programs, advice, and information contained in this book is at the sole choice and risk of the reader.

www.ingramcontent.com/pod-product-compliance
Lightning Source LLC
Chambersburg PA
CBHW071747170526
45167CB00003B/971